Little Star's Big Journey

An emotional regulation adventure.

By Alissa Dicke

For Brian, Lilah, and Rex

LilahAndRex.com
Copyright 2023 Alissa Dicke
All rights reserved.
First Edition
Printed in the USA

ISBN
979-8-218-35478-7

Little Star was silly and smart, but most of all was feeling curious.

You see, Little Star has been having a lot of big feelings lately.

It wanted to know more about what to do with such big feelings, so...

It went on an ADVENTURE across the Universe to find out more!

Little Star's first stop was Mercury.

It told Mercury all about feeling guilty when it knows it shouldn't do things, but does them anyway.

"Oh, I feel guilty at times too. We all do things we shouldn't at times," Mercury said.

"When I feel like I'm going to do something I'm not supposed to, I try to take a big breath in and a big breath out."

"I'm giving you a number 1 patch:

to help you remember it's okay to make mistakes and that big breaths can help!"

Next, Little Star floated over to Venus.

Little Star told Venus that sometimes it feels so angry it could explode.

"Sometimes I can get so mad I actually do explode and big volcanoes erupt," Venus replied.

"Then I remember that even if I get mad and explode, I am still loved."

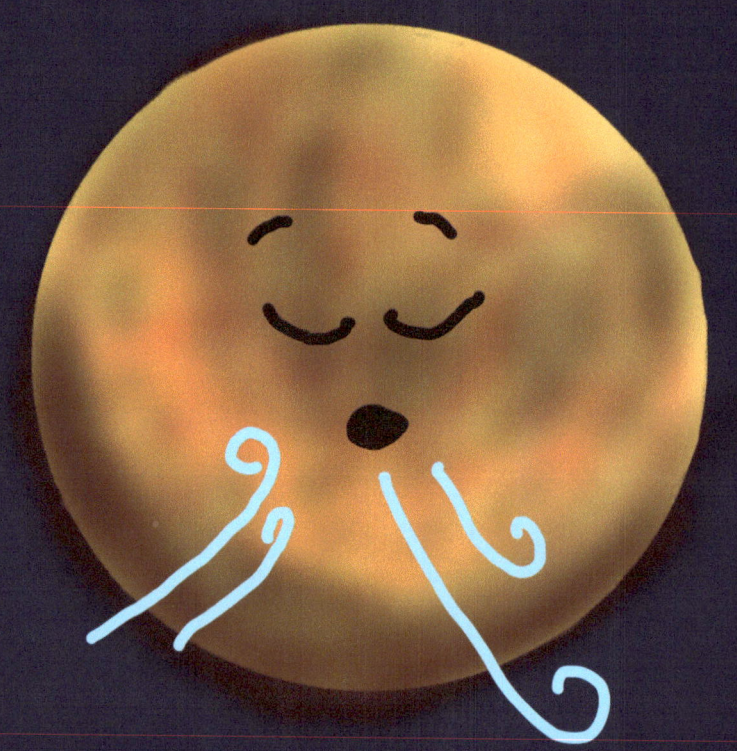

"I calm down by taking a big breath in and a big breath out!"

"I'm giving you a number 2 patch:

to remember that everyone gets mad at times; and that taking big breaths can help you find your calm!"

Little Star made its way to Earth.

It told Earth that it can feel really scared and anxious.

"It can feel scary when you're so little in this big Universe, but taking a big breath in and a big breath out can help you feel calm," said Earth.

"Sometimes I feel scared and nervous because I don't always know what will happen in the future. Deep breaths help me!"

"I'm giving you a number 3 patch:

to remember that it's normal to feel scared, anxious, or nervous sometimes. Breathing in and out can help you feel safer."

Little Star was starting to see a pattern and wondered what Mars might have to say.

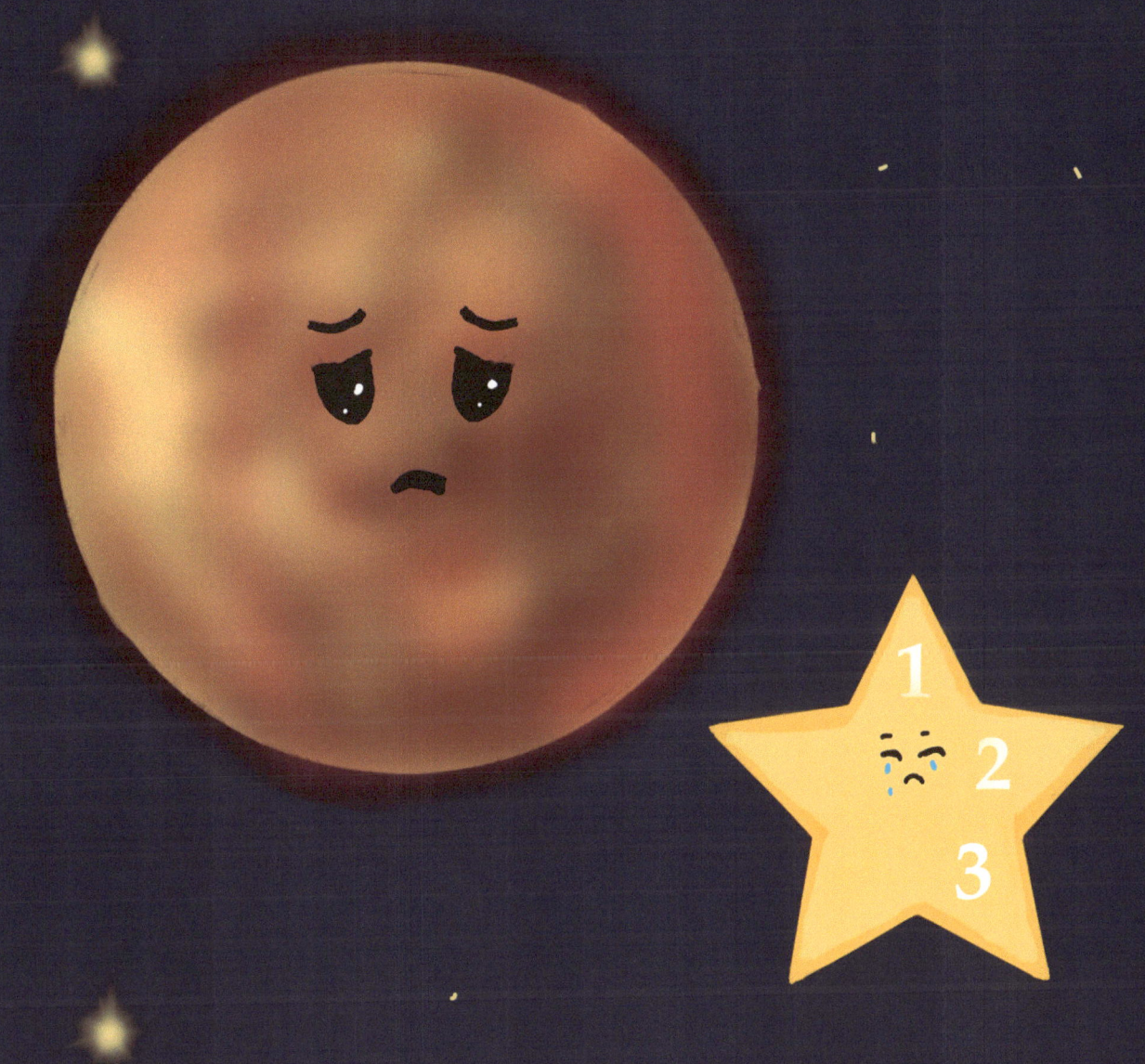

It told Mars that sometimes it feels really sad and wants to cry.

"Oh, sweet Little Star, it is always okay to cry," Mars said.

"Feeling sad is natural at times. Crying can help your body feel better.

Another way to help your body is to take big breaths in and out."

"I'm giving you a number 4 patch:

to remind you that being sad is normal and that breathing in and out can help you to feel a little less sad."

"Wow! All these planets know so much about feelings," thought Little Star.

"I wonder if Jupiter might know what to do when your feelings are so big that you can't contain them."

"Little Star, I know all about feeling big, stormy, and out of control," said Jupiter.

"That is why I've learned to take big deep breaths. They help me to calm myself down before screaming or hurting someone."

"I'm giving you a number 5 patch:

to remind you that you can always use breathing when you feel overwhelmed so you don't hurt yourself or someone else."

"Okay," thought Little Star, "that all makes sense. I need to remember to take big breaths in and let them out whenever my body has big feelings inside of it."

Nearby, Little Star could hear Saturn and Uranus talking about what they do to relax when feeling upset. "What do you do to help?" asked Little Star.

"Counting my rings really helps me!"
Saturn said.

"I count them: 1,2,3,4,5!"

"Counting helps me too," chirped Uranus.

"Spinning on my side I see things a little differently, so I count them backwards: 5, 4, 3, 2, 1!"

Little Star was feeling pleased about everything it learned, but wasn't sure if it could remember the whole process.

Suddenly, it bumped into Neptune! "I can help you remember the steps, Little Star!"

"First you take a deep breath in and let it out," said Neptune. "You do this 5 times, like the 5 patches you wear!"

"Then you count up from 1 to 5 like Saturn and then down from 5 to 1 like Uranus!"

Little Star was so grateful for the helpful reminder.

It was about to head home when it saw tiny Pluto floating around sadly.

"Are you okay?" asked Little Star?

"I feel sad and lonely," said Pluto. "I'm scared of how I feel. I'm angry.

I feel guilty that I'm mad because all the other plantes are bigger, while I'm just a dwarf planet. Mostly, I feel overwhelmed by all of these huge feelings."

Little Star knew just what to do!

"Breath in, breath out,
                        breath in, breath out,
breath in, breath out,
              breath in, breath out,
                          breath in, breath out.

Count with me: 1, 2, 3, 4, 5. Now backwards: 5, 4, 3, 2, 1."

"You are safe. You are loved!"

Pluto and Little Star felt so much better.

www.ingramcontent.com/pod-product-compliance
Lightning Source LLC
Chambersburg PA
CBHW042056050526
44107CB00110B/1195